C000007974

Born in Yorkshire in 1937, Tony Harrison is a poet and leading adapter and translator of classic drama, including *The Mysteries, The Oresteia, Phaedra Britannica* and *The Trackers of Oxyrhynchus* at the National Theatre. He was President of the Classical Association in 1987–88.

THE
COMMON
CHORUS

A Version of
Aristophanes'
Lysistrata

TONY HARRISON

faber and faber
LONDON · BOSTON

First published in Great Britain in 1992
by Faber and Faber Limited
3 Queen Square London WCIN 3AU

Photoset by Parker Typesetting Service, Leicester
Printed in England by Clays Ltd, St Ives plc

Originally published in the U.S.A. in The Agni Review (27), 1988

A CIP record for this book is available from the British Library

ISBN 0-571-14723-2

INTRODUCTION

Hecuba to Us

The one performance, the unique occasion, of an ancient Greek play may strike us now as an almost reckless encounter with the inexorability of transience, yet in its very uniqueness lies the secret of the glory of the continuously passing present of performance. We know, in proscenium terms, that once the curtain has risen it has to fall. The current obsession with televising and videoing stage performances almost inevitably undermines the true nature of the theatrical. But the play published here, conceived as it was for the National Theatre's Olivier stage, entered oblivion rather as unlucky players of Monopoly enter jail without passing GO. It entered the stream of oblivion without ever having been buoyed on it for even the brief unique performance that most Greek tragedies and comedies were designed to have.

My previous piece, *The Trackers of Oxyrhynchus*, although it later found a brief life on the same NT stage, had been originally conceived in this spirit, for one unique performance in the ancient stadium high up the slope of Delphi, a site considered by the ancients as the centre of the world. How differently the energies of performer and audience are concentrated if they know there is only one chance to give or receive the occasion. It was in this spirit too that the papyrus of the ancient play was in that version literally destroyed by fire, and it was in this spirit that the company prevented three rather peeved TV crews from filming what we all thought then would be the first and final performance, so that everything was committed to the care of memory, that last resort in the ruins of time. As Spenser wrote:

> For deedes doe die, how ever noblie donne
> And thoughts of men do as themselves decay,
> But wise wordes, taught in numbers for to runne,
> Recorded by the Muses, live for ay . . .

And elsewhere in *The Ruins of Time*:

> For not to have been dipt in Lethe Lake
> Could save the sonne of Thetis for to die:
> But that blinde bard did him immortal make
> With verses, dipt in deaw of Castalie:

All of us in *The Trackers of Oxyrhynchus* company drank literally the 'deaw of Castalie' before the performance at the sacred spring beneath the towering, red-hued Phaedriades at the beginning of the Sacred Way in Delphi. It was to give inspiration for that one occasion. But then surprisingly the play, although in a form altered for the specifics of the South Bank, was given more performances and what was intended to have been the last took place, again with local textual additions, in Carnuntum near Vienna, Austria, on 19 May 1990. Carnuntum was a former frontier post of the Roman Empire and the military base of three emperors, as commemorated on the label of the local Grüner Veltliner, wine grown by Josef Kock, the *Dreikaiserwein*, emblazoned with the heads of Marcus Aurelius (161–180), Septimius Severus (193–211) and Diocletian (284–305). Marcus Aurelius when he was in Carnuntum in AD 173, during his campaign to keep the marauding Marcomanni and Quadi respectful of the imperial border and stay on their side of the Danube, wrote, in his quieter moments what became Chapter Three of his *Meditations* in Greek. My original intention for the one performance in Delphi had been extended to Carnuntum, and on both sites there were associations of transience, in the spirit of which I had originally conceived the unique performance. At Carnuntum Marcus Aurelius was thinking about the inexorability of time and he wrote:

Hippocrates, after curing many sicknesses, himself fell sick and died. The Chaldean astrologers foretold the death of many persons, then the hour of fate overtook them also. Alexander, Pompeius and Julius Caesar, after so often utterly destroying whole towns and slaying in the field myriads of horse and foot, themselves also one day departed from life. Heraclitus, after many speculations about the fire which should consume the Universe, was waterlogged by dropsy, poulticed himself with cow-dung and died. Vermin killed Democritus; another kind of vermin Socrates.

Around that same time Pausanias, the physician from Asia Minor who wrote a guide to Greece in the second century AD, saw the ancient stadium of Delphi, where we had played our first performance. It must then have just been refurbished with marble from Mount Pentelicus by Herodes Atticus, who died around the same time as Marcus Aurelius. All that is left of that marble refurbishment are the chisel marks in the quarry from which the marble was taken. When Sir James Fraser, who edited Pausanias and checked on his descriptions at the end of the nineteenth century, stood on the site of the stadium he reflected that the marble had 'probably gone in the way of so many other ancient marbles in Greece into the lime kiln.'

Whenever I work at the National Theatre I usually walk to the South Bank from Clapham Common, and every morning as I walk along the Thames from Vauxhall I pass groups of Japanese tourists doing the same thing, taking pictures of each other from a position that gives them a shot of Big Ben in the background. The succession of clicks like an orchestra of clave wielders tuning up always makes me go forward to rehearsals committed to the essential transience of theatre. Theatre can only celebrate its presented moments by embracing its own ephemerality. In that is the glory of performance. Theatre has to be given and received at the moment of delivery. This is its essence. The mythologies of fame are mere yellowing calling cards. When the world famous conductor Herbert von Karajan died in 1989 his fellow conductor Sir George Solti observed: 'This year everyone talks about him. Next year it'll be 50 per cent less. The third year no one will say anything. This is the human fate, to be forgotten.' Heinrich Heine was appalled by the vision that he had of his *Book of Songs* being used by the grocer for packets into which to pour tobacco and snuff, rather as Ragueneau's wife, Lise, uses the manuscripts of her husband's poetic friends to wrap pastries and tarts in, in Act II of *Cyrano de Bergerac*. Addison, reviewing a show at Drury Lane for the *Spectator* in 1711, wrote of 'a dozen showers of snow which, I am informed, are the plays of many unsuccessful poets artificially cut and shredded for that use.' At the National Theatre stage door I came across a rehearsal draft of *The Trackers of Oxyrhynchus*, torn into three-inch squares, being used to write telephone messages on. And Jack Shepherd, who played Grenfell/Apollo in the production, told me that when he had been filming a legal drama the brief that his lawyer character carried was made up of old pages of a script of mine for a poem/film about death in Naples called *Mimmo Perella non è piu*. None of these fates are quite the indignity that Lord Chesterfield mentions in his letters of 1747 where, advising his son not to waste time, he cites the good example of a gentleman who purchased 'a common Horace, of which he tore off gradually a couple of pages, carried them with him to that necessary place, read them first, and then sent them down as a sacrifice to Cloacina.' The Egyptian *fellaheen* employed by Grenfell and Hunt in the excavations in *Trackers* used the papyri of Plato and Euripides as compost for their greens, and in the final version for the NT in 1991 the rubbish tips of the South Bank contained the poster, programme and text of the play being performed. The play contained the rubbished version of itself. Sometimes, walking from rehearsals, either via Covent Garden or via Waterloo, I came across other emblems of the ephemerality of theatrical endeavours I had been associated with. Walking past the now padlocked, dilapidated Lyceum I look up and take wry note of a piece of flapping poster saying 'The Best Show in Britain, no less' of the National's *Mysteries* that transferred there in 1985. Or walking through Cardboard City to catch the underground at Waterloo I see the now scarcely recognizable features of Edward Petherbridge and Sian Thomas and the fragmentary letters ON . . . IS of my own name on what was once a poster for my version of *The Misanthrope*, revived at the NT in 1989. On a concrete pillar in front of the crates and cartons that are the refuge of the homeless is the already disintegrating papyrus of a *Trackers* poster: . . . CKERS, it says. It is also heavily graffitied and in one place in smaller writing, to accommodate the message to the medium, the phallus of the leaping Silenus has been pencilled *Mrs Thatcher* – who has herself now entered the stream of oblivion meditated upon by Marcus Aurelius.

This contemplation of the ruins of time is a common theme in all literature and thought. As the philosopher George Santyana wrote: 'The spectacle of change, the triumph of time, or whatever we may call it, has always been a favourite theme for lyric and tragic poetry, and for religious meditation. To perceive universal mutation, to feel the vanity of life, has always been the beginning of seriousness. It is the condition of any beautiful, measured, or tender philosophy.' It is to find the meaning of suffering in such a context that Greek tragedy exists. And out of the same source comes the laughter of comedy and the celebration of the satyr play. Closer to our own precarious days the theme of transience was taken up by one who certainly helped us to become more fearfully aware of it. The 'father' of the atom bomb, J. Robert Oppenheimer, was thinking perhaps of a vista longer than the one his own invention shortened when he wrote:

> Transience is the backdrop for the play of human progress, for the improvement of man, the growth of his knowledge, the increase of his power, his corruption and partial redemption. Our civilisations perish; the carved stone, the written word, the heroic act fade into a memory of a memory and in the end are gone; this house, this earth in which we live will one day be unfit for human habitation as the sun ages and alters.
> (*Uncommon Sense*, 1984)

Certainly Oppenheimer's invention unleashed upon the world in 1945 made a great many people feel that we did not have to wait for the ageing of the sun for the earth to become unfit for human habitation. The American psychologist Robert Jay Lifton, who studied the survivors of Hiroshima, showed that when our sense of 'symbolic immortality' is undermined and threatened, as it was in the Cold War after 1945, then our 'confidence in the overall continuity of life gives way to widespread death imagery'.

It was into this new context of the old idea of transience experienced in the worst times of the Cold War nuclear confrontation that I chose to put the *Lysistrata* of Aristophanes and *The Trojan Women* of Euripides together as *The Common Chorus*. I imagined them played and performed by the women of the peace camp at Greenham Common for the benefit of the guards behind the wire who were defending the silos where the weapons of our ultimate extinction were stored. Nuclear weapons gave mankind what Hannah Arendt called a 'negative solidarity, based on the fear of global destruction'. Their presence also made us stare into the face of oblivion in a way unlikely to be redeemed in the memory of those whom Hecuba addresses as 'later mortals', and into whose hearts and songs she commits the suffering of her women at the end of *The Trojan Women*. As my Lysistrata is made to say in the text published here:

> In the Third World War we'll destroy
> not only modern cities but the memory of Troy,
> stories that shaped the spirit of our race
> are held in the balance in this missile base.
> Remember, if you can, that with man goes the mind
> that might have made sense of the Hist'ry of Mankind.
> It's a simple thing to grasp: when we're all dead
> there'll be no further pages to be read,
> not even leaflets, and no peace plays like these,
> no post-holocaust Aristophanes.

And no post-holocaust Euripides either! No Hecuba entrusting her story to the future. That moment in *The Trojan Women* was central to my understanding of how the tragedy and comedy produced within four years of each other might be played together. When everything has been taken away from the women of Troy, with their city in flames, the death of all their menfolk, the execution of the child Astyanax, it is left to the one who could be said to have lost most to seek for one last redeeming idea. Hecuba says:

εἰ δὲ μὴ θεὸς
ἔστρεψε τἄνω περιβαλὼν κάτω χθονός
ἀφανεις ἂν ὄντες οὐκ ἂν ὑμνηθεῖμεν ἂν
μούσαις ἀοιδὰς δόντες ὑστέρων βροτῶν   (1242–1245)

If we hadn't suffered we wouldn't be songs for 'later mortals'.
The song for later mortals is the tragedy being performed.
Hecuba addresses the Athenian audience of 415 BC across time
from an already mythical and long-ruined Troy. They are the
very 'later mortals' whose songs are Hecuba's redemption.
Every time the play is played through history in all its versions
the 'mortals' become 'later'. And we are the latest mortals now.
We are in that long line of 'later mortals' first addressed in 415 BC
as if from the present suffering of the Trojan Women of centuries
before. We are the latest mortals who guarantee that the
suffering was not in vain, and that the chain of commemorative
empathy is unbroken. *The Trojan Women* exit into the
imagination and memory of each audience whenever the play is
played. Hecuba leads her women into theatricality and into the
only redemptive meaning known to the pre-Christian world and,
I might add, to our *post*-Christian world. The pathos of her
address to us in our lateness in mortal history is all the more
precariously and transiently poised when it is made outside the
base where a destructive force is housed that will undermine
history and human memorialization permanently. It becomes an
appeal for the past not to be betrayed along with the present and
the future. As Lysistrata says:

> Since 1945 past and present are the same.
> And it doesn't matter if it's 'real' or a play –
> imagination and reality both go the same way.
> So don't say it's just a bunch of ancient Greeks.
> It's their tears that will be flowing down your cheeks.

In order to place the tragedy in this context I had to use the
contemporaneity of comedy to first establish the parallels and
allow the play to pass from Greenham to Greece and back in a
fluid way.

xi

If I am a serious witness of mutability and the ruins of time I have to confess that I believe that versions of ancient plays have to be redone for each new production. There exists the basic culturally deciduous network of stems and branches of the original, which itself changes shape through growth and atrophy, and there is also the foliage for each new season's versions. I live on yet another border of the Roman Empire, and often walk on the wall built by the Emperor Hadrian to divide the Romans from the barbarians. It has survived, or not, in various ways, ways that affect all monuments whether physical or spiritual. There are portions that have survived pretty well and can give a reasonable idea of the scale of the original enterprise. Then there are the bits of it – stones, milestones, altars, columns – from the wall and adjoining camps that have been recycled to become barns, farmhouses, pig-troughs, gate-posts, even church fonts and church pillars as at Chollerton. And there are sections – like the marble hewn from Mount Pentelicus to make the stadium seats in Delphi – which have gone into the lime-kilns, some of which you can still see, to become mortar for building new structures in a modern style, or fertilizer for depleted fields. Representing an ancient play uses all these processes. Sections can be revealed intact. Some are cannibalized as elements of modern structures, some transformed into bonding or fertilizing matter, generating new growth here and now.

Twenty years before I embarked on *The Common Chorus* I had done another version of the *Lysistrata* of Aristophanes for a group of student actors and village musicians in northern Nigeria in collaboration with the Irish poet James Simmons. The text is unperformable outside Nigeria and was responsive to the tensions that later erupted into a devastating civil war. Contemporaneity is essential to the serious comedy of Aristophanes. The political situation has to be mortally serious. His play was written in the twenty-first year of the Peloponnesian War that eventually destroyed Athens. And neither his play nor that of Euripides prevented it happening.

A women's peace magazine produced from Brighton in the 1980s called itself *Lysistrata*, and there was in its pages a reaching backwards to the suffering of the past meeting, if you like, the hands held out by Hecuba to the 'later mortals' from the ruined city of Troy. There was a sense expressed by these women and the women of Greenham that 'we are all interdependent, we are all responsible for each other, how delicate the strands, how strong the web'. Their historical empathy with the suffering of the past and their concern for the very existence of mortals later than themselves gave me the essential spirit to allow the play to move between Greenham and Athens 411 BC. If the tragedy I had wanted to perform with the comedy declared that remembrance was the one human redemption, then the comedy, in the spirit of the Peace Women's banners at the Cenotaph, declared that REMEMBRANCE IS NOT ENOUGH, and all their effort in the play is to prevent that dark, soul-rending effort of remembrance from becoming necessary once again in human history – if remembrance itself could survive the ruins of time in any Third World War. In that spectacular photograph of Greenham women dancing hand in hand in a circle on top of a missile silo I like to imagine both Lysistrata and Hecuba.

As Jeffrey Henderson tells us in his study of Aristophanic sexual imagery, 'of several words used to indicate the cunt whose basic notion is that of an opening or passageway, $\vartheta\upsilon\rho\alpha$ [= gate] is the most popular'. And it is outside the gate into the missile base that the Greenham women pitched their benders. On one notorious occasion the women padlocked the main gate. The hilarious sequence of soldiers and police trying to re-open the gate can be seen on the film *Carry Greenham Home*. I use the action to represent the occupation of the Acropolis in the ancient original and symbolically to represent the women closing the entrances to their bodies. As Henderson also points out, the most notable use of $\vartheta\upsilon\rho\alpha$ is in the *Lysistrata*, where it is used to mean the gate of the Acropolis and the gates of love.

Leaflets inviting women to come and demonstrate at Greenham by linking arms and forming a chain around the perimeter fence declared that 'we will turn our backs on it. Turn our backs on all the violence and destructive power it represents

. . .' In theatrical terms, by turning their backs on the base the women turn themselves towards the audience. Thus they are continually 'presented', as they would have been in the masks worn in the original ancient production. Also the Greenham women faced forwards in order to scrutinize those who pass by the base on foot or in cars for signs of support. In this way I could find a ready motivation for the actors to face outwards and play out to the audience. The Cruise missile bunkers had three metal shuttered openings, like the back of the Olivier stage. I had intended these to be raised at the end of the second play, *The Trojan Women*, to let out the headlights of the convoy bearing the missiles, blinding the audience before the final blackout.

I imagine the first play, the comedy, the *Lysistrata*, played with all its robust Aristophanic language as a direct response to the sexually abusive language that was continually directed at the women, especially when trying to sleep, by the guards at the wire. I spoke to Greenham women about this, and it is recorded by Caroline Blackwood in her book on Greenham, *On the Perimeter* (1984):

'I am so tired,' said Pat. 'We had such an awful night with the soldiers. They shouted at us all night. They just couldn't stop. It was sexual, of course. It's always sexual.'

Apparently many of the soldiers were under the impression that all the peace women were only camping round the base because they wanted to sleep with them. This was such a vain and deluded assumption, it was comic. Never had any group of men seemed less sexually desirable than the defenders of the Cruise missile when seen from the peace camps.

What is the matter with these soldiers, I wondered when I later heard them bellowing their horrible obscenities. Presumably they didn't carry on like dirty-minded schoolboys at home. Yet the peace women brought out everything that was sadistic and infantile in these men. The sex war that was raging on the perimeter was a very ugly and cruel one.

And, of course, behind these British guards, in the heart of the base, were the USAF personnel, recreating the comforts of the USA and singing the kind of songs that appeared for sale in a publication from the USAF 77th Tactical Fighter Squadron at Upper Heyford. The following are typical fare:

> I fucked a dead whore by the roadside
> I knew right away she was dead
> The skin was all gone from her tummy
> The hair was all gone from her head.
>
> And as I lay down there beside her,
> I knew right away I had sinned.
> So I pressed my lips to her pussy
> And sucked out the wad I'd shot in.
>
> Sucked out, sucked out.
> I sucked out the wad I'd shot in, shot in,
> Sucked out, sucked out,
> I sucked out the wad I'd shot in.

Or:

> I love my wife, yes I do, yes I do, I love her truly.
> I love the hole she pisses through,
> I love her ruby lips and her lily white tits,
> And the hair around her asshole.
> I'd eat her shit gobble, gobble, chomp, chomp,
> With a rusty spoon, with a rusty spoon.

Not all the songs are of masculine sexuality. There are battle cries also:

> Phantom flyers in the sky
> Persian pukes prepare to die,
> Rolling in with snake and nape.
> Allah creates but we cremate.

xv

North of Tehran, we did go
When FAC said from below
'Hit my smoke and you will find
The Arabs there are in a bind.'

I rolled in at a thousand feet,
I saw those bastards, beating feet,
No more they'll pillage, kill and rape
'Cause we fried them with our nape.*

I imagined such songs spluttering through the walkie-talkies of
the British guards at the wire, songs with a Budweiser slur,
coming from close to the silos where all the mod-cons of
Milwaukee were available so that the Americans didn't have to
feel they were actually abroad. We shall be glad to be rid of
such songsters and the weapons they brought with them.

Unfortunately the Quick Reaction Alert – which involved at
least one flight of nuclear-armed missiles being permanently in
readiness – is not a common category in the world of theatre, as
opposed to the theatre of war. There is no QRA at the RNT!
By the time various managements had lingered over this text,
the tension of a topical present and a tragic past had leached
away into oblivion. Thankfully the Cold War has ended and my
play has been marooned in its moment. The 'text', as
Tarkovsky said of the film script, gets 'smelted' into
performance. This text never went through that essential
smelting process. If I wanted to do *Lysistrata* now I might have
to begin again with a third and totally different version. To
recognize that a performance text has to be done again and
again is to acknowledge the transience, the flow, the
ephemerality of all theatrical realization. And it is in that spirit
that I have to acknowledge also that the time for this particular
version of the *Lysistrata* of Aristophanes has passed, with the
thankful ending of the fearful Cold War that produced it.
However, in July I received from friends in Dubrovnik *An
Appeal for Peace in Croatia*. It was written on the opening night

*nape = napalm

xvi

of a play: 'In these times of deafness in which the word that cries for peace and understanding has become inaudible, our Company is playing *Hekuba* by Marin Držić – the tragedy of a mother at the end of an absurd war.' Hecuba is once more committing herself to later mortals, aware of their imminent mortality. And where Hecuba is then Lysistrata isn't far behind.

Tony Harrison
Newcastle-upon-Tyne, October 1991

THE COMMON CHORUS

ACT ONE

Darkness. Last part of the night. USAF Greenham Common.
Spot illuminating a large letter C woven in the perimeter wire out
of rags, biscuit wrapping, coloured papers.

GUARD 1

(Standing behind the letter C)
>   Cock!

(Spot illuminates a letter N woven into the perimeter wire.)

GUARD 2

(Standing behind letter N)
>   Nob!

(Spot illuminates a letter D woven into the perimeter wire.)

GUARD 3

(Standing behind letter D)
>   Dick!

(Pause.)

GUARD 1

(To GUARD 2*)*
>   Can't spell you young uns of today.
>   Don't yer know that KNOB begins with a K.
>   NOB's got a K there in the front.

GUARD 2

Nah, daft ha'porth, K's for Kunt.

GUARD 1

Cock!

GUARD 2

Nob!

3

GUARD 3
Dick!

GUARD 1
Christ, but I could do with a screw.
Too long on this job, my balls are turning blue.

GUARD 3
I tell you, mate, doing this patrol
doesn't give a bloke much chance of hole.

GUARD 1
And if you spend too long on this fucking wire
you'll find someone's been at home poking the wife's
    fire.

GUARD 3
Back there the cunt's all Yankie and it's booked
so as far as fucking fucking goes you're somewhat
    fucking fucked.

GUARD 1
Ay, back there in the base there's bags of US pussy.

GUARD 2
Who cares where it comes from. I'm not fussy!
I'm a shagaholic, me. Hey I saw a real beaut
in a Buick, Dolly Parton tits, cute, real cute.

GUARD 1
Cock!

GUARD 2
Nob!

GUARD 3
Dick!

(One of the walkie-talkies at the hips of the GUARDS *begins to sound with the noise of Americans enjoying themselves. Males.)*

GUARD 2

Hey, listen, you can hear 'em boozing in their mess.

GUARD 3

The whole place, back there, 's like a miniature US!

GUARD 1

Bloody shopping mall, like downtown Milwaukee.

(More conviviality from the walkie-talkie.)

GUARD 1

(To GUARD 2*)*

For fuck's sake turn off that fucking walkie-talkie!

GUARD 1

Cock!

GUARD 2

Nob!

GUARD 3

Dick!

GUARD 1

When you go back there you're in for a surprise.
The stuff they've got. You won't believe your eyes.
And you won't believe how it's all so bloody clean.

(To GUARD 3*)*

Hey did you notice their 'rubber goods' machine?

GUARD 3

Durex, like?

5

GUARD I

No, that's the point, US rubberwear's
called Trojans. They call 'em Trojans, theirs.
I wanted to get a packet, like, just to have a look.
Would it take my 50p's, would it fuck.
The machine takes only US dimes and quarters.
I tell you I wouldn't take my wife or girl in.
Them Yanks, yer know, lock up your wives and
     daughters.
And it's all fucking dollars, mate, forget your fucking
     sterling.
Everything they've got back there's entirely Yank,
Yankee shops, Budweiser (deadly brew!) Yankee
     bank.

GUARD 3

Trojans? Funny name for spunkbags. What's it mean?
Never noticed the Yanks' rubber goods machine.

GUARD I

There's another sells Maintain 'with male desensitizer'
And some Yankee joker's drawn a sort of chart
for measuring, he calls it a 'cock-sizer'
and do yer know where the graduations start
for US 'Standard'? Two foot bloody six!
I tell yer, bloody Yanks, they're obsessed with their
     pricks.
Then under-bloody-neath it some swaggering shit's
scrawled 'Sub-standard sizes for sub-standard Brits.'

GUARD 3

Yer, funny. I suppose they think that that's a joke.
If I knew who'd written it I'd bloody bash the bloke.

Trojans?

(*To* GUARD 2)

6

Come on, Mastermind, you ought to know
you're the one with Geoger and Eng. Lit. (O).

GUARD 2

Troy were a city, wan't it, years and years ago?
Destroyed by fire, gutted, rubble, dust, debris.

GUARD I

Could they do that to cities in whatever it was BC?
Didn't have no Poseidon, Polaris, Cruise,
so what did those bloody Trojans use?

GUARD 2

Greeks, Greeks destroyed Troy. Chucked pitch-pine
firebrands, started a blaze. Fire does fine.

GUARD I

Ay, fire does fine. But all we have to do's
press a button and release one of their Cruise.

GUARD 3

Our Cruise, ours, it's supposed to be half ours
even though there are only the two superpowers.

GUARD I

The scientists since what's their names . . . the Trojans'
    day
have come up with fire concoctions in a very big way.

GUARD 3

They've concentrated fire so it can be hurled
at any place we're fighting anywhere in t' world.
What'll be next? They've perfected fire
and that's what we're guarding at this fucking wire.

GUARD 2

We can press the button and fucking fuck the lot
but the Greeks did alright without the stuff we've got.

7

GUARD 1

Ay, lad, we've come a long, long way
from rubbing sticks together to the fires of today.

GUARD 3

'istory's a pile of shit. I got F in mine.
I bet the first thing they did when Troy got took,
the first thing them Greeks did was fucking fuck.

GUARD 2

Well, I know the first thing that I'd do
after ten years on the firing line . . .

ALL

(*Singing*)

Shag the women and drink the wine
inky-pinky parlez-vous!

GUARD 1

Christ, but I could do with a screw.
I've been so long on this job my balls are turning blue.

GUARD 1

Cock!

GUARD 2

Nob!

GUARD 3

Dick!

GUARD 3

Yes, I think on that score the meeting is agreed!

GUARD 2

I'd like to be remembered for some heroic deed
enshrined in some historian of the future's words.

8

GUARD 3

Yer, how you guarded Greenham Common against a
   bunch of birds.

GUARD 2

George medal, Victoria Cross, DSO and bar . . .

GUARD I

Well guarding Greenham Common won't get you very
   far.
This isn't your World War I. You're hardly at the front
defending the Cruise Missile against a camp of cunt.

GUARD 2

There's no glory in soldiering any more,
we're just nannies to these nukes in a modern sort of
   war.
I'd sooner have been a hero in them old Trojan Wars
than stand here guarding missiles against a bunch of
   whores.
I'd sooner have been wounded in World War I or II
(not lost a leg or owt like that, a little wound would do)
gassed at Ypres, shrapnelled at the Somme
than listen to these bastards shrieking, Ban the Bomb!

GUARD 3

Don't know about gas attacks, but talk about pong
those bloody peace women don't half smell strong.

GUARD I

Yer, they don't have baths and they eat a lot of Heinz.
There's hot air in their gobs, and gas from their
   behinds.

GUARD 3

Two extremes innit that us lot are between
your hypershowered Yank and your Ms. Unclean.

Cleanliness is next to godliness is what they say.
Those Yanks have at least ten showers a bloody day.
Know nowt about godliness, but I know them loos
get a lot cleaner the nearer they are to Cruise.
And you know the filthy toilets that we have to use.

GUARD 3

Could be worse, old son, you might well have to shit,
like those poor bloody women do, over an earth pit.

GUARD I

I'll tell you summat that that word Trojan means
and it's a bit more serious than your johnny machines.
And it's nowt to do with your ancient overkill
put into Cinerama by Cecil B. DeMille.
1948. With Berlin still the trouble
and international tension starting to redouble,
your US brought their bombs

(*Out to* WOMEN)

                              that no-one's going to ban
and to meet the crisis drew up the masterplan
to nuke from bases, like this one here in the UK,
seventy Soviet cities with what was then your bomb.
Called War Plan Trojan!! and I dare say
that that's where they get their Trojan from.
To remind them when their thoughts might tend to stray
to a little screwing that they serve the USA.
And to let them know in the middle of a go
that they have a sacred duty to nuke old Uncle Joe.

(*Pause.*)

GUARD 3

So what were it about this fucking Trojan War?

GUARD 2

Some bit of skirt, I think, some fucking foreign whore
and half of bloody Greece perished at the front.

GUARD I

Ay, where there's trouble there's allus cunt.

GUARD 3

And look at these cunts in their bloody benders.
Greenham fucking Common what a place to send us.

GUARD I

If we have to stay awake, why should these cunts be
    kipping.
Let's wake 'em up. And when they look then we start
    unzipping.

GUARD I

Cock!

GUARD 2

Nob!

GUARD 3

Dick!

(*Then they begin chanting their abuse directed at the benders
where the Greenham* WOMEN *are trying to sleep.*)

GUARDS

Are you out there, Phyllis, come and give us a fuck?
Are you out there, Cynthia, come and give us a suck?

Camp-followers are yer, after military cocks
sucking off a sentry in his sentry box?

11

How would you like a nice shot of warm come
right down your tonsils, up your cunt, your bum?
The semen of he-men's superior to that
your stubby little hubby squirts into your twat.

Oh I can feel their little fannies start to ooze
when I unzip my flyfront and flash 'em my cruise!

Are you out there, Phyllis, come and give us a fuck
Are you out there, Cynthia, come and give us a suck.

(*Behind the* GUARDS' *taunting, repetitive abuse is a support
'choir' of American male voices coming from the walkie-talkies.*)

US VOICES

By Poseidon, those lousy Lesbian limey chicks
I think they're into dildoes not genuINE dicks!

Listen, you goddam father-sucking whore
don't you know what God has given you it for?

We didn't trounce your limeys back in 1776
to get the goddam run-around from a bunch of dykey
chicks.

(*The combined abuse of* GUARDS *and* US VOICES *rises to a
crescendo. There is a light inside a bender. From the bender
emerges the* GREENHAM *woman*/LYSISTRATA. *The abuse is
stilled. She places home-made improvised cocks on the wire in
front of each of the* GUARDS. *The* GUARDS *stand behind the large
cocks, which might be a cross between traditional Greek
phalluses and model Cruise Missiles. The* GUARDS *stand behind
the projecting cocks trying to ignore the fact that they look
ridiculous.*)

GREENHAM WOMAN/LYSISTRATA

A Bacchic debauch . . .

(Indicating GUARDS)

                               a booze-up as they'd say
would cause a ten-mile tailback on the motorway.
A pop

GUARD 3

piss-up

LYSISTRATA

            for Pan, with Uncle Sam
donating Bruce Springsteen and buckshee Babycham –
if that were the occasion the charas'd congest
the car-parks. Or a Coca-Cola Fest.
All night rock and complimentary bars
and Greenham would be overrun with gaggles of
   guitars.
All night rave-ups with bags of booze
and every gate at Greenham would have mile-long
   queues.
But now where are they? Where have the women
   gone?

GUARD 1

To a Lesbian vibratorthon!

GUARD 2

A jaunt with gigolos. A great sex spree.

GUARD 3

A genital joy-ride. Fucks for free!

GUARD 1

And Cruise-shape dildoes from the MoD!

(Enter GREENHAM WOMAN/KALONIKE.)

GREENHAM WOMAN/LYSISTRATA
Well, Kalonike, at least there's you.

GREENHAM WOMAN/KALONIKE
Now what's got into you. You look so down.
The Cosmo beauty column says you're not to frown,
you'll get crowsfeet and wrinkles . . .

LYSISTRATA
                       O so what?
You know women are a pretty rotten lot.
I'm pissed off with women if you want to know.

GUARDS
(*from behind wire*)
        Here we go, here we go, here we go!

LYSISTRATA
Maybe I am gloomy. Maybe there's good cause
and maybe we are, like *they* say, just a bunch of
    whores.
Maybe that lot are right in their horrible abuse.
We're good for one thing only. Otherwise no use.

KALONIKE
Let's be glad we're good for that.

LYSISTRATA
                    I made it clear
it was important so why aren't they all here?

KALONIKE
It's hard for a woman just to leave it all behind.
What'll happen to the kids preys on her mind.
She leaves notes on the fridge where *he* can't fail to see
on how to warm fish fingers for the children's tea.
Notes all over, you know a woman frets
in case *he* feeds the kids with Pal meant for the pets.

Piles of catfood with a note on all the lids;
this is for the pussies don't feed it to the kids.
Don't give Mary broccoli. It brings her out in spots.
Make sure Mark ties his shoelaces with proper knots.
Make sure that Samantha and Jonathan eat
their veggies up before they get a sweet.
David – dentist's! Thursday – Bonzo – Vet!
Notes with big red letters: DON'T FORGET,
Make sure Janet takes her pumps for gym.
Things really fall apart if they're left to him.
The list of DON'T FORGETS a woman sticks
on the wall's even longer than their

(*To* GUARDS)

                                        pricks!
All the billion details of the daily life
of your average unpaid slave, the British wife.
The billion details of 'domestic bliss'.

LYSISTRATA

Trivia! Trivia! Compared to this!

KALONIKE

What is *this*, then?

LYSISTRATA

A pretty big affair.

GUARD 3

(*From behind wire*)
We can provide that, you lot over there!

GUARD 2

Got just the ticket for you, haven't we, sarge?

GUARD I

Comes in three sizes . . .

15

GUARD 3
large . . .

GUARD 2
large . . .

GUARD I
and LARGE!

LYSISTRATA
Maybe it's still too early. Maybe.

KALONIKE
Too early, Lysistrata, you're telling me.
It's still only 411 BC.

LYSISTRATA
In that case the fate of Greece, all Greece,
which means both Attica and the Peloponnese
depends on women . . .

KALONIKE
O we're done for then!

LYSISTRATA
We're even more done for if we depend on men.
Every Spartan is going to die . . .

KALONIKE
Hurray, that means an Athenian victory.

LYSISTRATA
Everyone in Boeotia will be killed.

KALONIKE
But not the eels
they're absolutely scrumptious. Spare the eels.

GUARD 3

(*From behind the wire*)
>Do you notice what everything they think of's like?
>Now it's bloody eels! I bet that one's a dyke.

GUARD 2

Hey I've got something better than a Boeotian eel.
Come on over here, love, and have a little feel.

GUARDS

One day we'll have a weapon and that day isn't far
to destroy selective targets in the USSR,
zap the Bolshie's buildings (by Poseidon and by
>Cruise!)
but leave a few nice items that a feller could use
like all the fucking vodka and the fucking caviar
and a Rusky cunt or two for soldier's perks,
nutbloodycrackers, a Bolshoi ballerina,
and nuke these bloody Greenham Greeks but spare
the fucking ouzo and a few jars of retsina
and a few of the young ones in see-through underwear.

LYSISTRATA

(*To* GUARDS)
>Look, we're trying to pretend that this is ancient
>Greece.
>I wish you'd give us just a little bit of peace.

GUARD I

You'll get peace if we keep these weapons, pet.

LYSISTRATA

Those weapons haven't been invented yet.
We're still in the age of shields and swords.

GUARD I

Well they're not going to keep back your barbarian
>hordes.

17

LYSISTRATA

I wish you'd just shut up!

GUARD 1

Right, your Ladyship.
Listen, lads, lay off and they might do us a strip.

LYSISTRATA

Yes, your idea of theatre stops at striptease.
This happens to be a play by Aristophanes.
So try to be quiet and listen, PLEASE!

GUARDS

Here we go, here we go, here we go!

LYSISTRATA

We're NEVER going.

KALONIKE

(*Seeing the* WOMEN *approaching*)

They're all coming though.
The women from Anagyra. At least they've come.

GUARD 2

(*Whispering to other* GUARDS)

Anagyra's probably ancient Greek for Brum.

GREENHAM WOMAN/MYRRHINE

Are we early?

(*Frosty pause*)

Sorry, I'm late. OK?

LYSISTRATA

We need urgent action without delay
and you lot keep us waiting half the day.

18

GREENHAM WOMAN/MYRRHINE
I couldn't find my clothes. I had to creep
about in the dark. The children were asleep.
So here I am. What's the great idea?

LYSISTRATA
Wait till the Boeotians and the Spartans are here.
Then I'll tell you all my long-thought-out schemes.

GUARD 3
(*Out of corner of mouth*)
    Where's Boeotia?

GUARD 1
Bradford

GUARD 3
       Sparta?

GUARD 2
              I dunno . . . East
                 Cheam.

LYSISTRATA
(*Turning on* GUARDS)
    Look, if this were 1986
    and we were into international politics
    then the women coming here would have to be from
    the superpower countries who possess the BOMB.

MYRRHINE
Look, who's here now. It's Lampito.

GUARDS
Here we go, here we go, here we go!

LYSISTRATA
Welcome, Spartan sister.

19

(*Looks her over.*)

Mmm. Nice thighs!

LAMPITO

(*US accent*)
Yeah, it's the aerobics and the dancercise
we're into over there. Don't let your hands wander.
That ass comes from workouts with Jane Fonda.
She
(*indicates equally big USSR woman*)
uses anabolic steroids though.

USSR WOMAN
Capitalist hyena, that is not so.

LYSISTRATA
We're trying to stay in Greece, Ms. Lampito.

LAMPITO
OK, then let me introduce our . . . Boeotian friend.

GUARD I
How do you do, you've got a very nice rear end.

LAMPITO
She's from Corinth.

LYSISTRATA
Welcome.

LAMPITO
Did you call
this meeting?

LYSISTRATA
Yes, I did.

20

LAMPITO
OK then tell all.

LYSISTRATA
Yes, but first let me ask you, aren't you all sore
seeing your children's fathers going off to war?
All of us here, in one way or another,
as lover, wife, daughter, sister, mother,
have got to the point where we've seen
too many of our men fed to the war machine.

KALONIKE
My old man's been gone five whole months in Thrace.

MYRRHINE
It's seven since I've seen a man about the place.

LAMPITO
Mine comes home on leave with weapons and pack
and he's in at the front door and out the back.

LYSISTRATA
No lovers either. And the Milesians betrayed
the alliance and stopped the dildo trade.
Economic sanctions cut off our vibrators
and other D.I.Y. helps for man-starved masturbators.
So if I told you, that after much, much thought
I've hit on a solution, can I count on your support?

CHORUS OF WOMEN
1
I'd do anything.

ALL
And so would I.

2
Anything. Anything. I'd quite literally die.

3

I'll get the village church to hold a Bring & Buy.

4

I'll do anything, O anything at all.

5

I'll put up a petition in the village hall.

6

I'll make cakes to sell at the peace campaign stall.

7

I'll do a sponsored swim round the isles of Greece.

8

I'd give my right arm to bring about peace.

9

I'd do absolutely anything to make war cease.

10

I'll go canvassing support on my evenings free.

11

I'll do anything at all. You can count on me.

12

Tell me to do anything and I'll agree.

LYSISTRATA

Good! That's wonderful. I always knew
that I could count on every one of you.
So now I can tell you. I have a dream
that war will end, and a foolproof scheme,
Are you committed, are you forward-looking?
It's quite a sacrifice. It may come as a shock.
Let's have a show of hands, those who say yes!

(*All the hands of the* WOMEN *go up with simultaneous enthusiasm.*)

WOMEN

We're with you all the way. But tell us. We can't guess.

LYSISTRATA

For the sake of peace we have to give up . . . fucking!
And totally abstain, but totally, from COCK!

GUARD I

Let's check the other gates. I can't bear
hearing women, even Greenham women, fucking
swear.

(*Exit* GUARDS. *All the raised hands come down. The* WOMEN
back away.)

LYSISTRATA

Myrrhine, where are you off to? You've gone quite
white.

MYRRHINE

You know I've decided it's OK if men fight.

WOMEN

1

It's only a little war, Athens and Sparta.

2

It's not as if it's global, Lysistrata.

3

It'll be over by Christmas anyway.

LYSISTRATA

There's no such bloody thing as Christmas Day
Christ isn't born yet. It's BC four-eleven.

WOMAN 4

Not give up, cock. I love it, me. It's Heaven.
I'd rather walk through fire.

LYSISTRATA

(*To nearest* WOMAN)

What about you?

WOMAN 5

I think I'd rather walk through fire too.

LYSISTRATA

Bloody women! Maybe those back there

(*i.e.* GUARDS)

are right
and all we do want is what they shriek at us all night.
Lampito, Lampito, sister. It depends on you.

LAMPITO

Well, life's pretty terrible if you don't screw.
But peace has to come before sex, so, yes, OK.

LYSISTRATA

You're the only real woman here today.

KALONIKE

But if we do start living like a bunch of nuns
how will that make men lay down their guns?

LYSISTRATA

Their swords, dear, swords. But what's a name?
In essence all male weapons are the same.

LAMPITO

Remember one of Greece's chart-topping ditties
called 'Menelaus and Helen's Titties' . . .

24

(*Sings.*)

He'd wanted to give vent
to the rage that he'd long stored
but when he saw her bodice rent
he cast away his sword.

Before the longed for bosoms bare
he dropped his sword and stood,
and then he said: 'Your life I spare'
as she always knew he would.

Thousands of men went to their death
to win him back his bride.
Her titties took away his breath
and his sword fell to his side.

She opened buttons 1-2-3
and her breasts were half on view.
With all there was still left to see
how could he run her through.

LYSISTRATA

All we need's our perfumes, our pubic tweezers,
the outfits of the professional cock-teasers.
We'll be like their pin-ups on the barrack walls,
their wankers' fantasies, and make their balls
ache and turn blue till they can stand no more
and on the point of bursting they'll put an end to war.

LYSISTRATA
(*Picking up the 'Glamourwear' catalogue flung over the wire*)
Look at these undies our friends behind the wire
recommend for escalating sexual desire.

MYRRHINE
O, yes, I've seen their ads. I know them, Lysistrata,
plain cover catalogue with complimentary garter.

25

LYSISTRATA *and* CHORUS OF WOMEN

(*Reading from the 'Glamourwear' catalogue in the voice of the male morons who write the copy*)

1	Excita	*2*	Kitten	*3*	Camilla	*4*	Venus
5	Gypsy Rose	*6*	Siam	*7*	Tigress	*8*	Rosie
9	Lavinia	*10*	Natasha	*11*	Amazon	*12*	Wildcat
13	Madame	*14*	Maxine	*15*	LYSISTRATA!		

I

Loll about the lounge in a deluxe lingerie.
You'll have your geezer grovelling we guarantee.

ALL
ONE SIZE FITS ALL

2

Loll about your lounge in our deluxe lingerie
and his goggles will be glued on you and not page three.

ALL
ONE SIZE FITS ALL

3

Divinely delicious this explosive G-string. Wow!
Have the courage to wear this and he'll soon kow-tow.

ALL
ONE SIZE FITS ALL

4

Designer-style scanties exquisite art deco –
a dekko through the open parts. Go on have a go!

ALL
ONE SIZE FITS ALL

5

All men seek adventure. Go on give him some.
Open-nipple playsuits, colours: peach and plum!

ALL

ONE SIZE FITS ALL

6

Lounge about in this lace-fronted camisole –
more than a match for any feller's self-control.

ALL

ONE SIZE FITS ALL

7

Dress up in this one to serve his evening meal.
Tempting open crotch for extra man-appeal.

ALL

ONE SIZE FITS ALL

8

Open crotch panties in gold lamé –
wear it when he comes home tonight and make his day.

ALL

ONE SIZE FITS ALL

9

In enticing black with polka dots this half-cup basque
will set you up a treat for your titillating task.

ALL

ONE SIZE FITS ALL

10

Partially open panties give a hint of you know what.
Just the way men like their dinners . . . served up hot.

ALL
ONE SIZE FITS ALL

11

Order number 40A, colours: mauve and peach.
Gets to those other parts mere undies never reach.

ALL
ONE SIZE FITS ALL

12

A leotard in leopard with strategic scoops –
just the thing, darling, for tripping with the troops.

ALL
ONE SIZE FITS ALL

13

Black and glittering and very very glam –
come on heavy with him as the leatherclad Madame.

ALL
ONE SIZE FITS ALL

14

Slinky catsuit clings to every feline curve.
You'll get the jungle din-dins that you deserve.

ALL
ONE SIZE FITS ALL

15

Suspenders and black stockings with straight black
    seams
guaranteed (years of research) to gratify his dreams.

ALL
ONE SIZE FITS ALL

With little gusset buttons these pink silk cami-nicks
will get your geezer going in a couple of ticks.

ALL
ONE SIZE FITS ALL

Suggestive little bows untied with ease
and a strategic gold tassle for an extra touch of tease.

ALL
ONE SIZE FITS ALL

Camisole in lamé and lurex mesh –
flash your flesh in this and he'll soon get fresh.

ALL
ONE SIZE FITS ALL

This little crotchless scanty's trimmed with fur.
Tease your tired Tarzan. Groovy! Grrrrr!

ALL
ONE SIZE FITS ALL

Special occasion sporran, O och aye –
wear it G-string fashion and wait for fur to fly.

ALL
ONE SIZE FITS ALL

And this little number with a touch of class
shows half of your pussy and the whole of your arse.

LYSISTRATA

So that takes care of the uniforms we'll wear
Now gather round me. I want you all to swear
a solemn oath, never to fuck again
until war's been abolished by the men.

I swear all men, husband, lover or gigolo.

WOMEN

I swear all men, husband, lover or gigolo.

LYSISTRATA

If he comes near me with a hard-on will get a firm NO.

(*Pause*.)

If he comes near me with a hard-on, continue please.

KALONIKE

O all these approaching hard-ons make me weak at the
knees.

LYSISTRATA

I swear to live without it, entirely fucking-free.

WOMEN

I swear to live without it, entirely fucking-free.

LYSISTRATA

And slink about the lounge in the sheerest lingerie.

WOMEN

And slink about the lounge in the sheerest lingerie.

LYSISTRATA

Until his thing starts smoking he's so on fire.

WOMEN
Until his thing starts smoking he's so on fire.

LYSISTRATA
But not give in an inch to his passionate desire.

WOMEN
But not give in an inch to his passionate desire.

LYSISTRATA
And if he forces me against my will.

WOMEN
And if he forces me against my will.

LYSISTRATA
I won't fuck him back but just lie still.

WOMEN
I won't fuck him back but just lie still.

LYSISTRATA
I'll never ever wrap my thighs around his eyes.

WOMEN
I'll never ever wrap my thighs around his eyes.

LYSISTRATA
Or let him up the back however hard he tries.

WOMEN
Or let him up the back however hard he tries.

LYSISTRATA *and* **CHORUS OF WOMEN**
No blow-jobs, no hand-jobs, not even kisses
until he's going crazy for all he misses.

No slurping cunnilingus – cunnilingus, sister,
isn't that a bit of a tongue-twister –

No slurping cunnilingus, no soixante-neuf,
no togetherness of motion like the surfboard and the
    surf.

No soixante-neuf not even soixante-huit.
It's going in the freezer what he likes to eat.

No soixante-neuf, not even soixante-sept.
An unending hard-on's all he's going to get.

No soixante-neuf, not even soixante-six,
until he gives his promise to work for Peace.

No soixante-neuf, not even soixante-cinq
and strict surveillance so he doesn't wank!

No soixante-neuf, it's all soixante zero
until he stops behaving like a warlike hero.

No nothing, chum, closed legs and closed doors
until your mind is open to ending wars.

Your little prick's not going through its paces
until you've put an end to missile bases.

No generosity, no opening wide
until the world is free from impending genocide.

It's a headache (it's ballsache!) every night, my dear,
until you agree to a nuclear all clear.

From Athens to London, L.A. to Leningrad
if you've got a hard-on, mate, that's just too bad.

Take note Athenian Reagan, and Spartan Gorbachov
there's a female moratorium on having it off.

We're going to make sure that your balls turn blue
you'll suffer severe groinitis before we're through.
But when it's all over, you will only thank us
when we're making love together, and once more
you're in our beds, in a world with no war,
relieved of the strain of being war-mongering wankers.

(*Three* OLDER WOMEN *now cut the wire, and enter the base, and
occupy the sentry box, taking advantage of the absence of the*
GUARDS.)

LAMPITO
What are those women doing in the base?

LYSISTRATA
Protesting against the spiralling arms race.
Our sisters are taking over the sentry box
and we'll lock the 'Acropolis' with cycle locks.
And while we're doing that, off you lot trot
on the Spartan equivalent of Aeroflot.
We'll get things going here and while you're gone
influencing the Spartan Pentagon,
we'll lock those gates, and *these*

(*i.e. cunts*)

and locked they stay
until we Greeks of Greenham get our way.

WOMEN
They'll send the law. No chance. Them and us.

LYSISTRATA
Let them send the forces and the fuzz.
No threats, abuse, or anything they use
will make us open up till they abolish Cruise.

33

They may force those gates open. *These*
are staying firmly shut till every man agrees
never to make war, and only then
will we open our locked gates and let in men.

(*The* WOMEN *outside the wire place bike locks on the gates. One
of the three* OLDER WOMEN *who have occupied the sentry box
climbs on to the roof and unfurls a peace banner, maybe that one
which reads REMEMBRANCE IS NOT ENOUGH.* GUARD I
*appears, his walkie-talkie spluttering US obscenities. He rattles
the gates to no avail.*)

GUARD I

Now look what those bloody women have gone and
    done.
God! I sometimes wish they'd let me use my bloody
    gun.

(GUARD I *runs off. The* WOMEN *sing. Then from deep in the
base come the sounds of the First World War, the explosions,
ricochets, shells, gas rattles, Maxim guns. From the deep central
entrance we see moving towards us in slow motion the three who
are now to become three* WORLD WAR I VETERANS. *They are
wearing when they enter the gas-masks of World War I, British
issue. As they move downstage the sounds of World War I grow
fainter. They approach, remove their masks, and start marching
with rifles. As they draw near the gate they become old men, the
kind of* WORLD WAR I VETERANS *we still might see marching
proudly, if arthritically, past the Cenotaph on Remembrance
Sunday. When they stand behind the cocks on the wire, the cocks
detumesce and grow limp.*)

WORLD WAR I VETERAN I

Keep in step, old comrades, though now we're
    somewhat older
and these World War issue rifles are heavy on the
    shoulder.
First class fighting men we were, young heroic fighters

slowed down a little now by rheumatics and arthritis.
Not so chipper maybe when it comes to up a hill,
joints being rusty, but I bet you, with a bit of drill
we could present and slope and shoulder arms still.

WORLD WAR I VETERANS
1
Are we still up to giving these here Greenham wenches
a taste of what we gave the Boche in the Great War
   trenches?

2
Did our comrades suffer, did we trounce the Boche
to live to see these gals preaching pacifistic tosh?

US VOICE
And we didn't trounce you limeys back in 1776
to get the goddam runaround from a bunch of dykey
   chicks.

WORLD WAR I VETERANS
3
Did we volunteer for action, did we sign on, did we
   serve
to let women trespass on this masculine preserve?

4
Did we lose our youth, did we win against the Hun
to live to see the soldier made the butt of filthy fun?

5
We loved our dear old Blighty and the lasses we
   defended
but look now at these women here and how the
   country's ended.

We may look harmless now with our bad legs and
    arthritis
but once we stood erect and were proud to be good
    fighters.

We saw our comrades bloated and their bodies gnawed
    by rats.
You've no idea what war is, you pacifistic twats!

You go on about abolishing defence and guns
and you'll leave Britain open to tomorrow's warring
    Huns.

And after all our suffering and we got our demobs
we came back home to Blighty and found women in our
    jobs.

We came back home from the horrors of the trenches
and found women, wenches, manhandling our
    wrenches.

Pulling our levers, tightening our screws
and now, to cap it all, shrieking NO MORE CRUISE.

Were we gassed at Ypres, were we shrapnelled at the
    Somme
to have our daughters and grand-daughters yelling Ban
    the Bomb!

13

Did the lads who shared our billets lay down their
   precious lives
to have this military Acropolis occupied by wives?

14

If we only had our Maxim I tell you for a starter
I'd mow down that amazon Lysi-fucking-strata.

15

(Language, Drances,* lots of ladies out in front.
Don't let me hear any bollocks, fuck or cunt.)

16

If I were a lad again I'd be proud to serve the Queen
and I'd turn these women yeller with a few whiffs of
   chlorine.

US VOICES

Listen you old limeys to your Uncle Sam's advice –
get yourselves Cruise-missiles with a cunt-seeking
   device.

Failing that a canister of chlorine gas
from the good old days, and failing that your ass.

The trouble with you guys is the goddamn way
you turn all World History into Remembrance Day.

(*The* WORLD WAR I VETERANS *unpack a canister of gas.*)

WORLD WAR I VETERANS

Ay, gas, 22 April 1915
that was the date the Huns first used chlorine.
And only five days later, five fucking days
and us blundering and blind with eyeballs all ablaze

*A name in the original Aristophanes.

and comrades croaking from the Kraut's chlorine
27th of bloody April 1915,
women, bloody women have their pacifist pow-wows
over in the Hague with a bunch of fucking Fraus,
boatloads of the buggers, peacettes in petticoats . . .
I wish a Gerry sub had torpedoed all their boats.
Women, women, setting themselves up as being wiser
than us poor buggers at the front battling the Kaiser.
Could any idea be dafter,

2

dottier . . .

3

dopier

than peacettes in petticoats preaching their Utopia.

(*Cut to* GREENHAM WOMEN at Peace Conference.)

WOMEN
If not now, in heaven's name when?
When the world has killed off all of you men?
Brothers, husbands, sons into the jaws of War –
whatever then could we want a world of peace for?

WORLD WAR I VETERANS
You had to hold your pow-wow in the bleeding zoo.

WOMEN
Yes, and behind the bars were the wild beasts, you!

Remembrance Day and Cenotaph; that's something
   there won't be
in any city on the globe after World War III.

(*Silence.*)

WORLD WAR I VETERANS
I was there so why shouldn't I remember.
The Germans used it April, we tried it in September.

38

Ay, Ypres and Loos, I got myself gassed twice
once by the Germans then by our own device.

You don't have to tell me. I was there.
These clouds of green vapor rolling through the air.

Before my eyes conked out, that green cloud that I saw
made me think we'd seen the end of ordinary war.

It tore your lungs to pieces. It clawed your eyes.

US VOICES
Yeah, yeah, but get on with it, you guys.

WORLD WAR I VETERANS
Eyes that couldn't see, but couldn't stop weeping,
days of deep stupor and nightmare-filled sleeping.

We all had our eyes bandaged because of the gas
like see-no-evil bloody monkeys made of brass.

We marched in a crocodile, the one behind
the other in a long line of the blind.

US VOICES
Yeah, I'm sure you've got a lot of heroic tales to tell
but get these women out of our (I mean *your*) citadel.

(*As they fumble with their gas canister, the three* OLDER WOMEN
in the sentry box give them other things to remember.)

CHORUS OF WOMEN
I
Why can't they remember these would-be tough guys
they once had hardly anything inside their flies?

The little willies we washed and dried
now stiff and unyielding and courting suicide.

3

Why don't you remember the powder on your bots
then being tucked up with your teddies in your cots?

ALL

If Hist'ry retraced its steps along that bloody path
I could see you as my baby gurgling in your bath.

1

I see a blue romper suit with a white bunny tail
smeared with mud and blood and shit at Paschendaele.

2

I see my just bathed baby riddled by a hail
of Maxim gun bullets at Paschendaele.

3

I see the dimpled fingers learning Braille
because my boy is blinded at Paschendaele.

4

I see his naked body and his curly little head
burbling in his bath again but the water's red.

5

I see my baby in his bathtub with a blissful smile
but the bubbles all about him are blood and bile.

6

I see my baby with his little rubber duck
bobbing in a bathtub full of blood and muck.

7

I see my little baby with your milky breath
suddenly souring with the smell of death.

8

I see you my baby burping in your sleep
then coughing and choking with gas-filled lungs at
 Ypres.

9

Powdered in your nappy and the safety pin
suddenly a bayonet that gets rammed right in.

10

The nappy washed and rewashed, whiter than white,
full of grown man's shit as you run into the fight.

ALL

Why is my baby in bright red bath water?
I didn't wash him for this World War slaughter.
We don't bathe our babies for this bloody slaughter.
Why are our babies lying in this red bathwater?

11

And after I'd dried him and I'm putting on his vest
I see the shell-hole that's shattered his chest.

12

We clean the creases in his baby fat with a cotton bud
and find his later beer paunch oozing guts and blood.

13

Peeping through the bubbles his sweet little cock, it's
now the worm that winds in and out of his eye-sockets.

14

Is it only us remember these would be tough-guys
once had hardly anything inside their flies.

(*The* WOMEN *outside the wire have been responding to this from
the* WOMEN *inside the wire by a keening that began subdued and
now rises as they converge on the locked gates.*)

WORLD WAR I VETERANS
Hey look out the enemy's going into action.

WOMEN
What you see here's only a millionth of a fraction.

WORLD WAR I VETERANS
Out with the gas can, remember Loos.

WOMEN
And remember it turned out no bloody use.

WORLD WAR I VETERANS
Remember the boys we were in 1915
and give those enemies of Britain a whiff of our
    chlorine.

Right get ready. I've got the Hun in range.

WOMEN
What you seem to have forgotten's that the wind will
    change.
Like the new toys you've got stored in these bases
the stuff's going to get blown right back in your faces.

(*The* WORLD WAR I VETERANS *release the green cloud which envelops nobody but them. They choke in ancient Greek*:)

φυ φυ
ιου ιου
του καπνου

(*Their eyes are blinded. The smoke clears. The three* OLDER WOMEN *come from the sentry box and tenderly bandage the eyes of the* WORLD WAR I VETERANS. *They put a bunch of poppies in their hands.*)

42

WORLD WAR I VETERANS
We want to gas 'em and they give us bouquets!

WOMEN
To remind you of your mothers and your wedding days.

WORLD WAR I VETERAN 1
God knows it's true that I'd've gladly died
in battle to protect my mother and my lovely bride.

WORLD WAR I VETERAN 2
We were all of us ready to lay down our lives
to protect our little children and our helpless wives.

WORLD WAR I VETERAN 3
Even death wouldn't have been too much
of a sacrifice to make for my old Dutch.

(*They are older geezers now, tearful and pathetic. The punk girl who will later emerge naked as the image of* PEACE *goes through the hole in the wire and tenderly guides them into forming a 'crocodile', each with a right hand on the shoulder of the man in front, a famous World War I picture. She leads them slowly back into the depths of the base and the rest of the* WOMEN *keen for the dead in War.*)

(*Enter the* INSPECTOR *and two* POLICEMEN.)

INSPECTOR
Female crime. Every month shows an increase
both here in Britain and in ancient bloody Greece.
Is this what they call 'keening' for the horror of the
   BOMB?
Sounds like a million moggies wailing for a tom.
Sounds more like the way them Easterns holler
for that other feller they should nuke, the Ayah-
   bleeding-tollah.
Doesn't sound British. If you get my meaning.

43

A bunch of Pakis now, they suit your keening.
It sounds more like our coloured brethren's tones.
Not my sort of music. I prefer Tom Jones.
I don't mind demonstrations. Everyone is free
to express him (or her) self in our democracy.
But certain things are sacred. The Queen. Her subjects
who
lost their lives in either World War I or II.
They showed their banner REMEMBRANCE IS NOT
ENOUGH
at the service (shown on tele) at the Cenotaph.
In my humble submission that goes too far
whatever your political opinions are.
Women protesting! We've seen it all before.
They were even at it in the First World War,
chanting slogans, chained to bloody railings,
all this jiggery-pokery, women's 'wailings'.
1915 they tried it on then
bleating for Peace and undermining men,
who had a dangerous job to do.
But there weren't so many anti- in World War II.
Women were supportive. Women toed the line
when it came to facing Hitler in '39.
Well, gentlemen, I think we've got ourselves to blame
if women start this Greenham Common game.
By Poseidon, if you let go the reins
then they're going to end up in Peace Campaigns.
Some of my PCs, though I'm not a bloke to chide
display a certain laxness to the distaff side.
We do a lot of nights and while the cat's away
don't the little mice soon learn to bloody play.
Your intruder comes in a variety of guises
especially repair men with tools of all sizes.
Tupperware parties with the stress on *Tup*!
You never know what temptations might turn up.
I'm trained to spot the clues, and O I've seen her
casting dreamy glances at the vacuum cleaner.
Her and that salesman who egged her on to prove her

44

suction power stronger than his bloody Hoover.
We leave the gate wide open, wide,
and you wouldn't believe what walks inside.
Your postman whispering through the letterbox crack
'I've got a little something for you in my sack.'
Phoning the joiner, that's what they're all doing,
fitting the fixtures, a bit of the old screwing.
The plumber that comes round's not so bloody dumb
he doesn't know the pipes she wants him to plumb.
Carpet-fitter. Knock-knock! 'Come to lay . . .'
Little glances groinwards. Do I need to say?
There's two ways to deal with women: one's purdah
like our coloured friends, and the other's murder.
We let laxness in the home and when we're on the beat
they're giving someone else our little midnight treat.
We're out and about, enforcing British law
and they first learn whoredom and then denounce War.
If this is what happens when you treat her
like an equal, don't give her a millimetre
or she'll take six inches and it won't be yours.
Then they try to castrate us by stopping wars.
Domestic leniency, believe you me,
first it's sensuality, then it's CND.
First it's going out alone, with made-up faces,
then the next thing that you know surrounding missile
    bases.
One day it's taking classes, learning ancient bloody
    Greek
then it's aerobics and building a physique.
What's next you wonder, well one thing that's next
is our women getting missile systems hexed
with their witchcraft, wailing, all this, all this,
because in domestic matters men have been remiss.
You know we've given them far too free a hand
and the upshot of it is they'll destroy the land.
In my considered opinion they undermine the state
and as for Great Britain you can forget the Great.
It's my belief we're on the slipp'ry slope

because we've given women too much rope.
Now they've gone too far. They've cooked their goose.
Their necks are going to feel the tightening of the
    noose.
He's on our side. He's a bloke is Zeus.

Well, ladies, I think you should be knowing
that this is as far as Liberation's going.
Sorry to spoil your little fun, but from today
the only way you're going is Holloway.
I'm rather afraid that we're going to get tough.
The gentlemen of Britain have had e-bloody-nough!

(*To* LYSISTRATA)

You've locked these gates, madam. May we inquire
    why?

LYSISTRATA
Because the weapons in there bleed the country dry.

INSPECTOR
Locking the gates though. It doesn't make any sense.

LYSISTRATA
It's a protest against the money wasted on Defence.

INSPECTOR
O so we're a paid up economist are we, miss. I see.
The FT index is all Greek to me.
Tell me if you're an economist, miss,
about the money that gets wasted policing all this.
Have you ever thought about the cost to the nation
of policing your protest and your little demonstration?

LYSISTRATA

You won't need to do it once they withdraw
the missiles, and we've put an end to War.
The money stockpiled in that Acropolis . . .

INSPECTOR

Acro . . . Acro . . . is that some foreign lingo, miss?
English is all I ever need to speak.

LYSISTRATA

OK then, no more references to anything Greek!
The money represented by this wire fence
could be used on education if men had any sense.
The millions of pounds in your barbed wire barricade
could go on education here, or for Third World Aid.
The billions committed to your missile base
could go towards helping the human race.
These destructive systems waste enormous wealth
better spent on Housing, Education, Health.
The billions behind that guarded silo door
would feed more than 5,000 if we got rid of War.
Those millions in missiles and US personnel
could be spent on health care and making people well.
Those millions on missiles that you pour
along with human blood down the open drain of War.
Those millions, those billions stored in that concrete
could let the world's hungry learn to eat.
We protest against those billions that are poured
into payloads the nation can't afford.
Cash that's needed to house, feed, clothe, heal, teach.

INSPECTOR

Just open the bloody gate. Forget the Budget Speech.

LYSISTRATA

Inside blast-hardened bunkers housing Cruise
are millions the nation's being forced to misuse.
These palatial missile bunkers almost halve

47

the nation's resources and people starve.
Even if you never use your boyish toys
by taking from the needy deterrence destroys.
With Cruise missile money you could create jobs
for kids your kind will end up calling 'yobs'.
Their lives of unemployment don't make any sense
and the money needed is squandered on 'Defence'.
And by jobs I mean some profession other
than killing the sons of a Spartan mother.

INSPECTOR
Now you've lost me. Where the hell is Sparta?

LYSISTRATA
Where your payloads are pointing. The Peloponnese.

INSPECTOR
Didn't catch the last bit.

LYSISTRATA
                    Forget it, it's in Greece.
And if you want to know my name is Lysistrata.

INSPECTOR
Well – Miss, is it? – Lysistrata, or do we say Ms.?

LYSISTRATA
When I've finished with your armies it'll be *Dis*MS!

INSPECTOR
Your geography's confused, Ms. I do hope
your little ladies' commune's not into dope.

POLICEMAN
Shall we search them, Inspector? They look the type
that have their peace pow-wows with a hashish pipe.

OLDER WOMAN

I'll kick his knackers for him the cocky little devil.

LYSISTRATA

(*Restraining her*)

No, that would be descending to their male level.

(*to* INSPECTOR)

There's no confusion. *My* mind's clear
and there's no difference between there and here.
Since Hiroshima what we've done
paradoxically's to make the whole earth one.
We all look down the barrel of the same cocked gun.
One target, in one united fate
nuked together in some hyperstate.
So Greece is Greenham, Greenham Greece,
Poseidon is Poseidon, not just for this piece.
Not just all places, all human ages too
are dependent on the likes of us and you.
In the Third World War we'll destroy
not only modern cities but the memory of Troy,
stories that shaped the spirit of our race
are held in the balance in this missile base.
Remember, if you can, that with man goes the mind
that might have made sense of the Hist'ry of Mankind.
It's a simple thing to grasp: when we're all dead
there'll be no further pages to be read,
not even leaflets, and no peace plays like these
no post-holocaust Aristophanes.
So if occasionally some names are new
just think of the ground that's under you.
If we're destroyed then we
take with us Athens 411 BC.
The world till now up to the last minute
and every creature who was ever in it
go when we go, everything men did or thought
never to be remembered, absolutely nought.

49

No war memorials with names of dead on
because memory won't survive your Armageddon.
So Lysistrata! – (   )* – it's one name.
Since 1945 past and present are the same.
And it doesn't matter if it's 'real' or a play –
imagination and reality both go the same way.
So don't say it's just a bunch of ancient Greeks.
It's their tears that will be flowing down your cheeks.
So where we are, Greenham, ancient Greece,
doesn't matter. Their fates depend on Peace.
We've heard you men plan world-wide Apocalypse
and we went on serving dinner with sealed lips.
We went on sitting with our knitting in our laps
while you moved model missiles on your maps.
We heard the men's low murmur over their moussaka
and knew the world's future was growing a lot darker.
Serving the coffee we heard dark hints
of coming holocaust with after-dinner mints.
All this time supportive to the last
we nailed our colours to your macho mast.
I tried to discuss it with my husband, tried
to say he shouldn't vote for national suicide.
O, hello darling, did you vote Yea or Nay?
'Me, I'll always vote for Cruise to stay.
What's it got to do with women anyway?
Your province is knitting not national defence.'

INSPECTOR
O your husband, Mrs. Strata, seems a man of sense!

LYSISTRATA
A man of sense alright, if you can call
sense, wanting to destroy us all.
But male misgovernment grew more crass
and in the end we women couldn't let it pass.

*This parenthesis should be the name of the actress playing the role of
Lysistrata.

Crasser and crasser, week by bloody week.
We could have told you if you'd let us speak.
You've set the world on a collision course
 and still go on believing in masculine brute force.
We were driven finally out of sheer desperation
to devise a strategy to save the nation.
Perhaps it was the day we heard recruiters cry
that able-bodied men were in short supply.
And we decided that there was no point waiting
for men to end the war when it was escalating.
If men didn't want to staunch the flow of blood,
there was no choice about it, we women would.

(A big decision for an ancient Greek
not only not allowed to act, not allowed to speak.)

INSPECTOR
How can I stand here in the uniform of law
and listen to women, *women*, lecture me on War.
Us men sit and listen, us men submit
while *you* tell *us*, Hell, No, Shit!
Men give the advice and women take it.
Men enforce the law when women break it.
I'm a man. I say. You do. I wear the clothes
that give me authority and you wear those.

LYSISTRATA
Sexual identity, what a frightful bore
when the issue we're debating is the end of War.

(*To* WOMEN)

Take off his uniform. Who knows. Who knows.
Men are sometimes different without their clothes.

(The WOMEN *undress the* INSPECTOR *who is revealed to be
wearing women's underwear under his uniform.*)

(Reprising 'Glamourwear' song)

ONE SIZE FITS ALL!
Dressed like that, who knows, but you might find
you had a female side and change your mind
about war being a showcase for the male.
(If it were ancient Greece you'd wear a veil!)

LYSISTRATA

Though you're the stronger sex, play at the weaker
and be the listener while I'm the speaker.

LYSISTRATA *and* CHORUS OF WOMEN

We're going to dress up in that sort of groovy gear
until the men's cocks stick out right to here.

Eros. Eros. Bless your sexual co-workers.
Shoot your libidinous shafts from Piccadilly Circus.

When we've saved the country, we like you
will end up on a plinth as public statues too.

O Aphrodite, O Aphrodite,
bless me in my diaphanous nightie
and my scanties crucially see-through
and I'll end up a statue the same as you.

We'll use erotic means to stop the flow of blood
and end up a public plinth labelled MOTHERHOOD.

This is the time, you are witnessing the birth
of a new love of country meant to save the Earth.
MATRIOTISM, and no-one has to die,
MATRIOTISM destroys patriarchy,
MATRIOTIC women save the earth.

It'll be good to see an end of soldiers in town
pushing trolleys loaded with Newcastle Brown.

Like commandoes on a mission you see them clear
the entire supermarket of its stocks of beer.

Their supermarket trolley loaded dangerously high
with the only sort of product they ever seem to buy . . .

Tins of Newcastle Brown, six-packs of Tartan
to give them lots of courage to fight against the Spartan.

Being buffers between the British and the US bases
affects their behaviour too in public places.

A bit belligerent and bloodshot from the booze
clomping into pubs and shops, and jumping queues.

And everyone too timid to ask them to desist
because *a*. they're aggressive and *b*. extremely pissed.

Whooping after women, with crude view halloo
full of the inky-pinky parlez vous.

Frightening other shoppers, scaring the cashier
clanking with their purchases in military gear.

Their purchases are only ever one thing: BEER!

INSPECTOR

Ach, what do you know of war, you web-concocting
    spiders?

LYSISTRATA

Everything! We are the child-providers!
All war's victims started life inside us.
To improve your understanding let's reverse
roles even further. Here!

(*Gives* INSPECTOR *a 'baby' to hold.*)

                              Take this child to nurse.
Hold the baby close, see how it feels
then maybe reconsider women's peace appeals.
Hold the baby in a close embrace
and know why women hate your missile base.
No, let's not laugh at him. His female side
might help to hold us back from genocide.
Hold the baby closer, croon, try to be tender.
Break out of your imprisoning stiff gender.
Don't sing to the child that dark male lullaby;
Bombs-away-baby, you're going to die.

Mother the cannon-fodder for your War!

INSPECTOR
(*Breaking down*)
Stop it. Stop it. That's too much. Please, no more!

LYSISTRATA

Then imagine waiting while the one you bore
the cannon-fodder of the future for
is away from home himself and at the War.
Worse off than those women who have known
a little love and now are left alone,
's the girl, approaching womanhood, who waits
while war is wiping out all likely mates.

INSPECTOR
Men grow old, you know, not only you.

LYSISTRATA
Yes, but look what happens when you do.
Bald, decrepit, toothless a man still gets
into the knickers of nubile nymphettes.
But for a woman once she's over the hill . . .

INSPECTOR
(*Rising to the occasion*)
Well, if a man can get a hard-on still . . .

GUARDS
(*From behind the wire*)
Here we go, here we go, here we go. Hooray.
Three cheers for an old man's hard-on's what we say.

LYSISTRATA *and* WOMEN
Your hard-on's the first sign of *rigor mortis*
an exit sign not one of excitation.
Death's Helltons and Death's Dusthouse Fortes
have their hot-lines open now for reservation.

Your obsessions with these cocks of yours,
their blood-bloated hardness, length and size
has always led us blindly into wars,
because you can't bear *not* to seem tough guys.

It's time to die while you can still have flowers
and a memorial carved in stone with touching verses.
Time to be buried properly before the superpowers
make bulldozers and black plastic bags our hearses.

While they still make the cedar and oak coffin
I'd book one now while firms are still supplying
to carry you and your poor hard-on off in
before the superpowers start us panic dying.

Die now while there's a time for tears and waking
with generous shots of whisky and cold ham.
The kind of funerals the Powers have in the making
is one mass grave for all of Birmingham.

So go and die while there's still time for weeping
beside the spot you chose for wife and self
while there's a time for grandsons to be keeping
their granddad's photo on the mantleshelf.

Here's some poppies from the people who still care
and baklava for the watch-dogs at the dock.
Here's cash to give to Charon for your fare
to ferry you across Death's Holy Loch.

Go and die while there's still time for strewing
carnations on your coffin while folk cry.
A time to mourn before War's total ruin
blows flowers and the folk into the sky.

Go, die while you can keep your male illusion
your cock-bound fantasies of right and wrong
before corpses fuse in chaos and confusion.
Go, and we'll see you off with a sad song.

(*The* WOMEN *'bury' the* INSPECTOR, *and the cock is buried in a
separate coffin. The* INSPECTOR*'s coffin is made from two
discarded police riot shields so that it is like Snow White's glass
coffin.
The* WOMEN *bear off the two 'coffins', the* INSPECTOR *in the
see-through coffin and the cock in another.*)

GUARDS

(*From behind the wire*)

I

There's more to this than meets the eye.

There's more to this than meets the eye.

There's more to this than meets the eye.
And we suspect a

Spartan

German

Russian SPY!

There's more to this than meets the eye.

There's more to this than meets the eye.

There's more to this than meets the eye.

ALL

These Greenham women have got to be
infiltrated by the KGB!
I don't believe what we've just seen.
They've been infiltrated, they must have been.

There's more to this than meets the eye.

There's more to this than meets the eye.

There's more to this than meets the eye.

The

1
Spartan

2
German

3
Russian infiltration

getting at the weaker sex to overthrow the nation.

1

There's more to this than meets the eye.

2

There's more to this than meets the eye.

3

There's more to this than meets the eye.

1
Ruskies,

2
Gerries

3
SPARTIES!

Subversive left wing parties,
something subversive's been and got 'em.
Shock 'em to the senses, show 'em your bottom!

1

There's more to this than meets the eye.

2

There's more to this than meets the eye.

There's more to this than meets the eye.

ALL

To reassert the glory of the uniformed male
let's flash it at 'em and watch 'em quail.
Rise to the occasion, on the word of command
present your naked cock in your right hand.
Your country needs you, the Fatherland calls
for brave heroes who've still got all their balls.

(*The* WOMEN *begin to re-enter.*)

When they look this way, flash it at 'em quick,
all they hang around here for's a bit of dick.
Flash it at 'em, fellers, and make the fuckers flinch.

WOMAN

(*Not looking*)
    If you took your hand away we could see the whole
      inch!

(*The* WOMEN *go into their benders. The light is failing. There are
shadows and torches inside the benders as the* WOMEN *begin
settling down to sleep. There is a sense of intimacy, solidarity,
friendship, sisterhood.*)

WOMAN 1

You know if we flashed back
the guards would die of a heart attack.
If one of us went out and stood in front
of one of them, and went and flashed her cunt,
the poor little lad would get such a shock
it would soon shame him to put away his cock.

WOMAN 2

Their foulness though it makes me weep.

WOMAN 3

They'll go on all night and won't let us sleep.

WOMEN

Good night! Good night! You know it feels so good
and so secure, in spite of them, this sisterhood.

GUARDS

There's more to this than meets the eye.

(*They 'flash' as one of the* OLDER WOMEN *pokes her head out of
the bender.*)

OLDER WOMAN

Well, I hope there's more to that than meets the eye!

(*Darkness. The torches in the benders go out. The orange lights
of the base fade down. Blackout.*)

ACT TWO

A later morning.

LYSISTRATA

I can't keep them here. They're all in need of it.
Prick-sick the lot of 'em. And ready to quit.
They seemed so dedicated but they desert
because their randy bodies are on Red Alert.
Women behaving like those lot say they do –
any little dodge to get themselves a screw.
Those foul-mouthed lots behind their barricade
are right: all women want is to get laid.
Every little dodge, every devious trick,
anything at all to get a dose of dick.
Every kind of lie, every sneaky stratagem
to get a stiff six inches into them.
Every fraud you've heard of, every ruse,
more concerned with cock than campaigning against
   Cruise.
They're all so randy, so screaming for a screw
it can't be long before the Peace Campaign is through.
I found one by the Orange Gate trying to hitch
a lift back to London, the treacherous bitch!
One by the roadside skirt half up her thigh
luring lorry drivers into a lay-by.
There was even one about to sneak off to the bar
where the US personnel take R & R.
Women! Women! Traitors, they betray
our campaign sisterhood for one quick lay.

(WOMAN 1 *enters*.)

Here's one now, trying to slip away.
Morning! Off somewhere in a hurry, pray?

WOMAN I

Yes. 'er yes, I'm sorry, have to I'm afraid.
I just thought of the milkman. He has to be paid.

LYSISTRATA

It's not important. You've got to stay.

WOMAN I

I'll give him what he wants and come back
    straightaway.

(*Enter* WOMAN 2.)

WOMAN 2

Shit! I've just remembered, the cat! The cat!

LYSISTRATA

(*To audience*)
    Do you know how many times I've already heard that?
    I know your pussy's dying for some Whiskas, dear,
    but you and your pussy are staying right here.

(*Enter* WOMAN 3.)

WOMAN 3

I forgot to turn the gas off. Honestly.

LYSISTRATA

And we're trying to turn off World War III.

WOMAN 3

I only need a night to check. I don't want to quit.
I only want to go back for a bit.

(*Enter* WOMAN 4 *pretending to be in labour*.)

WOMAN 4

OOO the contractions! They've begun.
Phone for the ambulance. Don't stand there, run!

LYSISTRATA

Nine months' gestation in a single day!

WOMAN 4

OOOO the baby, the baby's on its way.

(LYSISTRATA *knocks on the swollen belly of* WOMAN 4 *and there is a hollow metallic sound.*)

LYSISTRATA

It's hard and hollow, and makes a funny noise.

WOMAN 4

Hard and hollow, just like all the little boys.

(LYSISTRATA *reaches under* WOMAN 4*'s clothing and pulls out a helmet from World War I, as seen on the* WORLD WAR I VETERANS.)

LYSISTRATA

And what's this, this relic of World War I?

WOMAN 4

I was going to use it to bathe my little son.
You know the Greenham spirit: improvise.

LYSISTRATA

I know it's a pack of monstrous, shameful lies.

(*Enter* WOMAN 5.)

WOMAN 5

I don't want to seem alarmist but I've seen a snake.

(*Enter* WOMAN 6.)

WOMAN 6
Those bloody owls all night keeping me awake.
I haven't slept for weeks. Too-whit-too-bloody-whoo.

LYSISTRATA
What the hell's got into all of you.
You want your men. But imagine THEY
are equally desperate for a lay.
Just think of them restless and rigid in their beds
with only one thought always in their heads:
How long, O Lord, how long before the next screw.
So, please, persevere. Let's try to see it through.

(*Enter* KINESIAS PAEONIDES/DICK DIXON *with a little boy*.)

KINESIAS
In comes I. Great God Almighty.

(*Brandishes cock*)

Look how I'm afflicted by Aphro-bloody-dite.

LYSISTRATA
O goddess of all sexual desire
keep on adding fuel to the fire.

(*To* MYRRHINE)

Right, tease him. Serve him only the hors-d'oeuvres.
But that's the only course you're allowed to serve.
A little kiss, maybe, but nothing more
just remember the solemn oath we all swore.

MYRRHINE
OK! OK!

LYSISTRATA
And I'll help to whet
his appetite while you put on your glamour set.

KINESIAS
OOOO I've got testicular tetanus, lock-cock.
Inches lust-winched to yards and hard as rock.

LYSISTRATA
Who goes there, friend or foe?

KINESIAS
Me!

LYSISTRATA
A man!

KINESIAS
Doesn't it show?

LYSISTRATA
Well if you're a man you'll have to go.

KINESIAS
I want to see Myrrhine before I do.

LYSISTRATA
You want to see Myrrhine and who are you?

KINESIAS
Her husband, Kinesias (Dick Dixon) is my name.

LYSISTRATA
Say no more. It's preceded you . . . your . . . fame.
Everything reminds her. Your wife's
obsessed with you. I saw her salivate
over a still unopened crate
of a certain fruit consignment labelled Fyffes.

When we women chat, Myrrhine's little boast
is Kinesias (Dick Dixon) the man with the most.

KINESIAS

Call her!

LYSISTRATA

Do I get a tip, some *quid pro quo*?

KINESIAS

(*Waving his cock.*)
You can have the tip of this before you go.

LYSISTRATA

I'll bring her.

KINESIAS

          Quick! I tell you chaps my life
has lost all meaning since I lost my wife.
The living room's a shambles. I sit on the settee
that used to hold us both and now holds only me,
so lonely that I've started talking to the TV.
Food that I used to love has lost its savour.
She was, I realize now, what gave it flavour.
Her love and care were the bouquet garni
that put my appetite for living into me.
Don't know where my clothes are. Can't get dressed.
I tell you I've never felt more depressed.
It's a dog's life doing your own cooking,
all the fucking housework, then no fucking.
All I can think of is this . . . this . . . growth.
The bed's not big enough to hold us both.
We sleep in separate beds. I'm not able
to have my breakfast sitting at the kitchen table.
It's getting out of hand. Jerking off won't work.
It's got too wide to get a grip on it to jerk.
It's very painful this phallic hypertension.
Had to have my trousers built with an extension.

66

The be-all-and-end-all of my being's THIS . . .
this . . . this . . . this . . . Edifice.

MYRRHINE

(*Off, arriving*)
He says he loves me but it's all an act!

KINESIAS

(*Indicating cock*)
Isn't this clear demonstration of the fact.

MYRRHINE

No, I'm off.

KINESIAS

(*Desperate, pushing forward* LITTLE BOY)
No, please, Myrrhine,
look, the little lad, he's so much thinner.
It's for your little child that I appeal.

(*Gives* LITTLE BOY *a poke.*)

LITTLE BOY

Mummy!

KINESIAS

It's weeks since he had a proper meal.
Or wash. Look at him. He's filthy. Look.

MYRRHINE

Can't his father bathe him, learn to cook?

KINESIAS

Come back, my darling, at least for your son.

MYRRHINE

(*Drawing nearer*)
>A mother's work is never done –
>by men!

KINESIAS

>God, she's so much more, much more
>attractive than she ever was before.

MYRRHINE

(*To* LITTLE BOY)
>O let me give you a big kiss.
>Your dad's a proper brute neglecting you like this.

KINESIAS

>Listen, why do you pay any heed
>to this bunch of dykes. Look at me. In need!
>The whole house, everything's gone to pot.
>You wouldn't believe the shambles.

MYRRHINE

>   O so what!

KINESIAS

>All the little knick-knacks that you had
>the dogs have broken them.

MYRRHINE

>   That's just too bad!

KINESIAS

>I bet you miss our bed. God Al-bloody-mighty
>you used to be pretty into Aphrodite.

MYRRHINE

>I'm not coming back till you men negotiate
>an end to the war.

KINESIAS
When it's decided by the State
we'll do it.

MYRRHINE
Well, you'll stay in that state till they do.
Till then, I'm not coming home to you.

KINESIAS
What about a quickie at least before I go?

MYRRHINE
I can't say I don't want to, but no! NO!

KINESIAS
Come on, I know you, always oversexed.

MYRRHINE
Here in front of the lad, whatever next?

KINESIAS
(*To* LITTLE BOY)
Here, come here, darling.

(*Whispers.*)

Scram!
I want a word in private with your mam!

(KINESIAS *gives the* LITTLE BOY *a toy wooden sword, or pistol,
to play with. One of the* WOMEN *coaxes the 'weapon' off him and
exchanges it for a dove on a stick. He goes off, playing with it, at
first bearing it like a peace protester then suddenly making it into
a dive-bomber with appropriate noises.*)

KINESIAS
Now come on, love, lie down, lie down.

MYRRHINE

Where?

KINESIAS

Any-bloody-where! Right here! I don't care!

MYRRHINE

But, Kinesias, Dick, I did swear a solemn oath.

KINESIAS

Bugger it. This thing's bigger than us both.

(KINESIAS *moves towards her*.)

MYRRHINE

Wait! A groundsheet!

KINESIAS

The bare earth'll do!

MYRRHINE

O the ground's not good enough for you.
You big, strong, impulsive thing, so butch.

(MYRRHINE *leaves for groundsheet*.)

KINESIAS

She was always one for that little extra touch
of comfort. Shows her love.

(MYRRHINE *returns with groundsheet*.)

Up with your bum!
I'll just slip my clothes off, then I'll come.
Be with you in a jiffy. Damn, O damn!
Forgot the mattress.

KINESIAS
I'm terrific as I am.

MYRRHINE
I want you to be comfy!

KINESIAS
A kiss! Just one.

MYRRHINE
There!

(*Kiss*)

KINESIAS
O wow! Go on then, run, run, run!

(MYRRHINE *leaves.* KINESIAS *lays back on ground. Cock rises.*
He sits up again.
Enter MYRRHINE *with mattress.*)

MYRRHINE
There we are, my love. Just like a proper bed.

(KINESIAS *lays back, up rises the cock. He sighs with*
anticipation.)

MYRRHINE
Getting my clothes off!

(*Thinks*)

Something for your head!

KINESIAS
I don't want a pillow.

MYRRHINE

I'd like one though.

(MYRRHINE *leaves*. KINESIAS *sits up and looks woefully at his cock*.)

KINESIAS

Poor cock, you're starving. The womb service is slow.

(*Enter* MYRRHINE *once more with pillow*.)

MYRRHINE

I think that's everything.

(*Puts pillow under* KINESIAS.)

There you go!
I'll just slip off this bra.
A blanket!

KINESIAS

NOOOO!
I don't need the Bayeux Tapestry, a four poster,
a Goblin Teasmade, a pop-up toaster,
a morning alarm call, a bedside book.
All I need, Myrrhine, is a FUCK!

(MYRRHINE *leaves*.)

MYRRHINE

I'll be back in just a couple of ticks.

KINESIAS

(*To cock*)
Poor cunt-craving junkie where's your fix?

(MYRRHINE *returns with blanket*.)

72

MYRRHINE
Up! Up!

KINESIAS
Up! Up! Can't you bloody see –
I've been up since seven. *He's* been up since three!

MYRRHINE
You'd like some perfume?

KINESIAS
No more, PLEASE, no
more!

MYRRHINE
You used to insist on it before.

(*Goes for perfume. Returns.*)

Hold your hand out. A little to please me.

KINESIAS
Pooh, Chanel bloody No. 2 if you ask me.

MYRRHINE
O that's the one from Rhodes. That wasn't very clever.

(MYRRHINE *makes to leave.*)

KINESIAS
NO, it's the most perfect perfume ever.

(*Sloshes it over himself, then gulps the rest down.* MYRRHINE
leaves.)

KINESIAS
God rot Gucci, Nina Ricci and Chanel.
Fuck all parfumiers. They can go to Hell.

(MYRRHINE *returns*.)

MYRRHINE
This is so much better, smell.

KINESIAS
No more
little treats. I've got a better one in store.

MYRRHINE
OK, darling. I'll just slip off my shoes.

(KINESIAS *lies back. The cock rises. He sighs*.)

But you will remember to campaign against Cruise
and work towards a Spartan Armistice?

KINESIAS
I'll seriously consider it.

(*Sighs*)

Ah bliss!

(*Pause* KINESIAS *sits up*. MYRRHINE *has gone*.)

Slowly the conviction dawns. O God she's gone
and left me with the hardest bloody on
I've ever had in the whole of my damned life.
At the crucial moment stood up by the wife.

(*He sings a lullaby to his cock, which he nurses like a baby*.)

Cock-a-bye baby,
cock of my life,
it doesn't seem likely
that you'll lay the wife.

74

GUARD 1

Cock-a-bye, cocky
but don't despair.
We know where you'll find
professional care!

GUARDS

Bollocks weren't created to suffer such a strain.
There's a limit to the agony a man's cock can sustain.

KINESIAS

O my knob is throbbing like a dynamo!

GUARD 1

Ay, we had a gander and fancied a go.

GUARD 2

Weren't bad in her undies. Quite a show.

GUARD 3

You could tell she were a proper bastard though.

(*Enter the* HERALD, *a dual twin of USA/USSR.*)

KINESIAS

Hello, hello, no, don't tell me. I know you two lads
you're the well-known ancient fertility ads.

HERALD

I am a herald, a preparatory ambassador
sent to initiate *détente* in the Cold War.

KINESIAS

Détente? If your concern is PAX
why the weapons peeping from your macs?
Or is it an affliction of the bollocks?

HERALD

The man's a lunatic, by Castor and by Pollux!

KINESIAS

But the evidence is there. Your balls do swell.

HERALD

My credentials. An emblem of authority.
A sort of staff of status in the Spartan nation.

KINESIAS

Gettaway with you. You can't fool me
We're all suffering from similar inflation.

(*Shows his cock.*)

Join the club. How are the Superpowers?
Proper cock-up is it, just like ours?

HERALD

Women! Women! Even my old missus
with KEEP OUT signs on all their orifices.
Not so much as a distant whiff of cunt
until we've voted for disarmament.

KINESIAS

Now I see it. It's universal then
this female conspiracy against us men.
Contact your governments. Tell them this:
Urgent send envoys to sign an Armistice.
The problem's universal. All we need to do's
open up our flies for a frank exchange of views.

HERALD

(*Leaving*)

No more SS20s. No more Cruise.

76

GUARD I

Bloody marvellous how they get under your skin.
The one thing about women is you never win.

GUARD 2

With 'em, without 'em, they drive us round the bend.
But don't you think this hostility could come to an end?

GUARD 3

We'll be kind to women, if they'll be kind to men.
How about it, ladies, no hard feelings then?

(*One of the* OLDER WOMEN *goes up to the youngest of the*
GUARDS, GUARD 2.)

OLDER WOMAN

Well, if you ask me, you looked very silly
trying to impress us with your little willy.
What about your mother? What would she have
    thought
seeing her son doing something of that sort?

O poor lad, you've got something in your eye!

GUARD 2

Yer, I think it's a bleeding fly,
something like that, or a speck of dirt.

WOMAN

(*Through wire*)
        Here, let me see. O yes. It must hurt.
        Look at me.

(*Pause.*)

            Look up at the sky.
        Look at me.

77

(*Pause.*)

> There!
>> There's no need to cry.

GUARD 2
(*Cross but crying*)
>> You've made it start watering, poking my eye!

WOMAN
(*Dabs his eye through the wire*)
>> I'll kiss it better, love.

(*Kiss kiss*)

> There!

GUARD 2
(*Backing off in acute embarrassment*)
>> Hey, you daft old bugger, don't you dare!

(*Enter the* AMBASSADORS.)

WOMAN
> Here come the ambassadors from both blocs
> bridging the gap between them with their cocks.

AMBASSADOR 1
> We are following our pieces to make Peace.

AMBASSADOR 2
> Enough rigidity. We want release.

LYSISTRATA
> I'd better act. Or in a couple of ticks
> they'll be tickling one another with their pricks,
> or getting up one another's bum,
> or blowing one another into Kingdom Come.

Gentlemen, without further hindrance, let or pause
PEACE emerges for the past of human Wars.

(*From the central entrance deep in the bases emerges* PEACE, *a
naked* GREENHAM WOMAN – *the one we last saw leading the
blinded* WORLD WAR I VETERANS *back into the depths of the
base. Her body is smeared with ash and blood as if
commemorating August 6, Hiroshima Day, or the anniversary of
Nagasaki. The* WOMEN *with pebbles and stones – out of which
they make a commemorative cairn – set up a rhythm to bring
*PEACE *downstage. Three times* PEACE *stops and the rhythm
stops. In the pauses we hear wolf-whistles coming from as if deep
in the heart of the bases.* PEACE *carries rolled up at this stage a
banner of the Peace movement depicting the world in very bright
coloured cloths over which is a disarmament symbol. When she
reaches the front of the stage she unfurls the banner. The
disarmament symbol on the world continues with* PEACE's *legs.
Where the arms of the symbol divide is exactly over the cunt of
*PEACE.)

LYSISTRATA
Bring them together. Don't bully or cajole
like some pissed husband desperate for his hole.
Be gentle with them. They should be led
not like machos trundling women into bed.
If they won't join hands as friend to friend
then lead them by the part they do extend.

(*The* AMBASSADORS *are led to the centre where* PEACE *stands.
Their cocks form an inverted V, that parallels the disarmament
sign. They at once try to glance over the banner to the naked
*PEACE *behind.*)

LYSISTRATA
Before we finish off I'd like to say
that it's August 6th, Hiroshima Day,
which is why you see Peace smeared with ash and
blood.

79

Yes, we'd all go back to 411 if we could.
It would have been good to turn back the clocks
and have a little romp with padded cocks.
The patriarchs of 1986
still battle for world power with their pricks.
Hiroshima, that world-transforming blast
makes it that much harder to reclaim a simpler past.
Besides if *Lysistrata* was put on then
every part would have been played by men.
So for the sake of theatre let's retrace
our steps. Forget this is a missile base
patrolled by these poor lads for the USA
and let's get back to our prenuclear play.
This is the Athenian Acropolis
where Athens and Sparta sign the Armistice.
So end the hostility between you two.
Why don't you make peace? What's stopping you?

AMBASSADOR 1
We'll make peace but these

(*Points to areas on the world above the breasts of* PEACE.)

are our spheres
of influence, and his country interferes.

AMBASSADOR 2
We'll make peace, *if* it's understood
that this territory

(*Points to area of the world above the cunt of* PEACE.)

stays ours for good.

GUARD 1
Time for Peace feelers. I wouldn't mind.

GUARD 3
She had nice tits, and a gorgeous behind.

(GUARD 2 *is silent. The* WOMEN *begin bringing thermos flasks and sandwiches to offer the* GUARDS *through the wire. The* OLDER WOMAN *gives food first to* GUARD 2.)

OLDER WOMAN
You look a bit peeky, guarding all night.
Here, aren't you hungry, have a bite.

From our secret stash of Harrods hampers
here's smoked salmon and vintage champers.

Food from Fortnum's we have stashed away
hidden in the bushes to celebrate today.

(*All they have to offer is a thermos and sandwiches in plastic bags.*)

You know we get the odd crown-pattern wrapped food
    parcel
a brace of pheasants or a grouse from Windsor bleeding
    Castle.

(*The* WOMEN *are unfurling all their bright banners.*

Enter a DRUNK GEORDIE SOLDIER *returning for duty at the base. He's very drunk and carrying what's left of a six-pack of Newcastle Brown.*)

DRUNK GEORDIE SOLDIER
What's going on here, then? A bloody party,
a booze-up between your Athenian and your Sparty?

GUARD I
You're not supposed to come in through the front.

81

Howay, let us in, man. Divvn't be such a cunt.
I've got to be doing your job tomorrow.
Do you blame us if I want to drown my sorrow?
Politicians of the world. My advice is this:
before you negotiate, go on the bloody piss.
They all look fucking wonderful. Even your wog
when you're looking at him through a haze of grog.
Know what I mean, pet? Here have a swig.
I'm not your average male chauvinist pig.
Howay, pet! I'll tell you something: booze
is the surest way there is to banish Cruise.
Know what, hinny, when you've had a few,
they all look lovely, even some of you.
Ruskies, Yanks, Jocks, Japs, Chinks,
they're all one big family after a few drinks.
I'll tell you something else: The Brotherhood of Man,
the Brotherhood of Man's in this Brown Ale can.
Get everybody pissed. And just you watch.
World Harmony's a matter of your beer and Scotch.
It works like that with birds. After fifteen pints or so
some old slag can look like Marilyn Monroe.
I've drunk with your Greeks, ancient and today's –
they all look lovable through an ouzo haze.
I'll bet them ancient Greeks swigged a lot of wine
then went bopping to bazoukis and singing *Auld Lang
    Syne*.
I'll tell you something. And you'll think I'm barmy
or just a bloody bastard 'cos I'm in the army,
but I've got a soft spot in my heart for CND
(Now I wouldn't want anybody quoting me . . .)
Everybody, everybody has a right to say
that your Cruise should go back to the USA.
I bloody hate myself. I bloody hate
having to stand on guard at this bloody gate.
Give us a kiss, and I'll tell you something more.
I hate myself and I bloody hate War.
Honest, cross my heart, when I'm bloody pissed

I think even the Ruskies have a right to exist.
Been pissed with Gerries, they're very nice chaps
not Schweinhunds when you've shwigged enough
    schnapps.
Now I'm going to have a few jars with the Yanks.
They're looking after us, they deserve our thanks.
Off to their Bob Hope Center, very nice place
tucked away at the heart of this missile base.
I'm telling you it's all so neatly planned
you'd think this desolation was Disney-bloody-land.
They're alright, Yanks, not bad for a laugh.
But I tell yer their beer is fucking naff.
Budweiser! Women's beer! I wouldn't give a glass
of that piss ('scuse my French) even to wor lass.
Tell you what, I'll toss you a few over the wire.
You can wash your faces in it, or douse your fire.
I'll bring you some six-packs from their PX store
and you can drink to disarmament and the end of war.

(SOLDIER *lurches through gate towards the depths of the base.*)

LYSISTRATA

Now it's all over, we should celebrate
the glad reunion of mate with mate.
We hereby restore
sex, and abolish War.

Take your partners, hug and kiss,
the world's drawn back from the abyss.
Dance, celebrate creation
saved from man's annihilation.

GUARDS

War, it'll only survive in old soldiers' stories.
All our heroic deeds, our military glories.
If war's finished then we'll never get our gongs.
War'll go into museums where it, perhaps, belongs.

83

The Greeks resisting though outnumbered by the
   Persians.
Memories like that though help to form a nation.
Yes, the Greeks have their Marathon and our version's
standing alone against the Nazi until our Uncle Sam
came to help us out a bit and outstayed his invitation –
Marathon, the Somme, Dunkirk, Suez and Vietnam.
Gives me a funny feeling though that War's
gone the same way as the bloody dinosaurs.
Museums and old movies, miles of celluloid
of Coventry or Dresden, Hiroshima, Hanoi
have bombs dropped on 'em and systematically
   destroyed
and Peace will make them seem as far away as your old
   Troy.

Hey, but wait a minute we'll be unemployed!

The only buttons anybody's gonna press
aren't the ones to nuke us into Nothingness
but Fast Forward Wind as *nostalgie de la boue*
brings us endless re-runs of World War I and II.

I betcha after a few years of World Peace
all the old war films'll be on re-release.
You watch the figures on the home video charts
when the rush of War Nostalgia actually starts.

We'll have to show the kiddies what they've missed
or else they won't believe that such things could exist.

History'll come to a dead end. I mean
wars, that's all history's ever been.

Well from now on it's taken a new turning
and there'll be a very different tale to be told.
From now on the only fires you'll see burning
are those in living rooms to keep away the cold.

Goddess of childbirth send increase,
send new babies from tonight's embrace.
Entrust the future to us here in Greece
standing in for all the human race.

Artemis, Goddess, we beseech you, bless
everything that you create
brought back from the brink of Nothingness
and bless mate reconciled with mate.

Goddess, who wants the world to go on turning,
who wants the grass to grow, the trees to bud,
turn men's hearts away from bombs and burning,
turn men's hearts away from dust and blood.

Goddess walking the high mountain slopes
walking space and time from ancient Greece,
look down and bless our new fragile hopes
rooted in a future of eternal peace.

Goddess of sex, you from whom
comes the child, the tree, the flower,
bless the fruit of the glad womb
saved at the dark eleventh hour.

Britain's not a dancing nation
not like the ancient Greeks before us.
But the joy of reprieved creation
moves us as a common chorus.

Dance, dance, join hands and glide
in tune with the rhythms of the earth
released from the curse of genocide
pulsing with rebirth, rebirth.

(*As the* WOMEN *dance, the* DRUNK GEORDIE SOLDIER *emerges
from the depths of the base erratically pushing a shopping trolley
laden with Budweiser beer. He proceeds to lob the cans over the
wire making grenade noises whistles and explosions. A* WOMAN
*cuts a large hole in the wire so that they can be passed through.
The* WOMEN *start drinking them.*)

WOMAN
(*To* GUARDS)
We've sung our song for the end of Wars.
Come on, fellers, now it's your turn. You sing yours.

(*The* GUARDS *shuffle with embarrassment, then stand to
attention and to the tune of* Rule Britannia *sing*:)

GUARDS
Bless the women,
the women lead the way,
women, women, women, women lead the way.

Thank you ladies,
Lysistrata was a scream
but a

1
stupid

2
Stupid!

3
Stupid!

86

ALL

DREAM.
Well, that's enough of ancient Greece.
We've got to live in our own age.
Tell those who won't join in your peace . . .

(*They raise three walkie-talkies out of which comes a repetitive*
US VOICE.)

US VOICE
We'll nuke 'em back to the Stone Age.
We'll nuke 'em back to the Stone Age.
We'll nuke 'em back to the Stone Age.

(*As this point enter a real* POLICE INSPECTOR *with* POLICE *and*
BAILIFFS *who proceed to destroy the women's benders.*)

INSPECTOR
Right, I'm nicking the lot of you for breaching the
peace!

(*Blackout.*)